★ It's My State! ★ ★ ★ ★ ★

ARIZONA
The Grand Canyon State

Kathleen Derzipilski, Amanda Hudson, and Kerry Jones Waring

Cavendish Square

New York

Published in 2016 by Cavendish Square Publishing, LLC
243 5th Avenue, Suite 136, New York, NY 10016

Copyright © 2016 by Cavendish Square Publishing, LLC

Third Edition

Website: cavendishsq.com

This publication represents the opinions and views of the author based on his or her personal experience, knowledge, and research. The information in this book serves as a general guide only. The author and publisher have used their best efforts in preparing this book and disclaim liability rising directly or indirectly from the use and application of this book.

CPSIA Compliance Information: Batch #WS15CSQ

All websites were available and accurate when this book was sent to press.

Library of Congress Cataloging-in-Publication Data

Waring, Kerry Jones.
Arizona / Kerry Jones Waring, Kathleen Derzipilski, and Amanda Hudson.
pages cm. — (It's my state!)
Includes bibliographical references and index.
ISBN 978-1-62712-476-8 (hardcover) ISBN 978-1-62712-479-9 (ebook)
1. Arizona—Juvenile literature. I. Derzipilski, Kathleen. II. Hudson, Amanda. III. Title.

F811.3.W37 2016
979.1—dc23

2014049271

Editorial Director: David McNamara
Editor: Fletcher Doyle
Art Director: Jeffrey Talbot
Designer: Joseph Macri
Senior Production Manager: Jennifer Ryder-Talbot
Production Editor: Renni Johnson
Photo Research: J8 Media

The photographs in this book are used by permission and through the courtesy of: Lawrence Freytag/Getty Images, cover; George H.H. Huey/Alamy, 4; Eu Toch/Thinkstock, 4; Juniors Bildarchiv/Alamy, 4; Gaertner/Alamy, 5; Asya Babushkina/Shutterstock, 5; Rick and Nora Bowers/Alamy, 5; Beboy/Shutterstock, 6; Martin M303/Shutterstock, 8; Tom Bean/Alamy, 9; Westgraphix LLC, 10; Kevin Ebi/Alamy, 11; Don Kates/Alamy, 12; Kevin Schafer/Alamy, 13; Francesco R. Iacomino/Shutterstock, 14; File:Lowell Observatory 2009.jpg/Wikimedia Commons, 14; Simeon87/ File:Pima Air & Space Museum - Aircraft 23.JPG/Wikimedia Commons, 15; Jami Garrison/Thinkstock, 15; Tom Bean/Alamy, 16; warnsweet/Shutterstock, 17; Bob Gibbons/Alamy, 19; Rick and Nora Bowers/Alamy, 20; VibeImages/Thinkstock, 20; Mira/Alamy, 20; Grand Canyon NPS photo by Michael Quinn/File:Water-thrifty "Bonsai" Tree Along the Grand Canyon Rim 8025 - Flickr - Grand Canyon NPS.jpg/Wikimedia Commons, 21; Genevieve Vallee/Alamy, 21; Cynthia Kidwell/Shutterstock, 21; Cacophony/File:Canyon de Chelly White House.jpg/Wikimedia Commons, 22; Zack Frank/Shutterstock, 24; George H.H. Huey/Alamy, 25; Skip Higgins of Raskal Photography/Alamy, 27; Corbis, 28; Dennis MacDonald/Alamy, 29; North Wind Picture Archives/Alamy, 31; Andwhatsnext, aka Nancy J Price - http://andwhatsnext.com/File:Vulture-gold-mine-maricopa.JPG/Wikimedia Commons, 32; Pictorial Press Ltd/Alamy, 33; Buddy Mays/Alamy, 34; R1/Alamy, 34; Photodisc/Getty Images, 35; Tim Roberts Photography/Shutterstock, 35; Sun City: David South/Alamy, 41; rshantz/Alamy, 42; The Image Bank/Getty Images, 44; Hemis/Alamy, 46; Hulton Archive/Getty Images, 48; Sony BMG Music Entertainment/Getty Images, 48; Allstar Picture Library/Alamy, 48; Lana Harris/AP Photo, 49; ChinellatoPhoto/Shutterstock, 49; Getty Images, 49; Accurate Art, 50; Tomas Abad/Alamy, 51; Tomas Abad/Alamy, 53; © 2007 Chuck Feil/PanTerra Gallery, Bisbee, AZ, 54; Courtesy Lake Havasu Striper Derby, 54; Karol M/ File:Hoop Dancer8.jpg/Wikimedia Commons, 55; Christian Petersen/Getty Images, 55; Nagel Photography/Shutterstock, 56; rabh images/Alamy, 58; Getty Images, 60; Robert Harding Picture Library, Ltd/Alamy, 61; Joe Raedle/Getty Images, 62; RAVEENDRAN/AFP/Getty Images, 62; FEMA Photo Library/File:FEMA - 39840 - Official portrait of Department of Homeland Security Secretary Janet Napolitano.jpg /Wikimedia Commons, 62; Mark Wilson/Getty Images, 63; Ken James/Bloomberg via Getty Images, 64; Jim West/Alamy, 66; Susan E. Degginger/Alamy, 67; Transtock Inc./Alamy, 68; Caro/Alamy, 68; Susan E. Degginger/Alamy, 69; Bill Bachmann/Alamy, 69; photogal/Shutterstock, 70; Getty Images, 71; Christopher Santoro, 74; Michael Runkel/Alamy, 75; Nina Henry/Thinkstock, 75; Christopher Santoro, 76 (seal and flag).

Printed in the United States of America

ARIZONA
CONTENTS

A QUICK LOOK AT

★ State Flower: Saguaro Cactus Blossom

Saguaro blossoms grow on the tips of the arms of the saguaro cactus. The cactus, which grows only in the Sonoran Desert, blooms from mid-May to mid-June. The white blossoms typically open at night and close the next day. Some of the flowers develop into sweet, juicy fruits full of tiny seeds.

★ State Tree: Palo Verde

Palo verde is Spanish for "green stick." The tree gets its name from the green bark on its branches and trunk. In the spring, yellow flowers cover the trees. Creatures such as rock squirrels rely on the palo verde seeds for food. The trees grow in sandy areas and rocky hillsides throughout the Sonoran Desert.

★ State Bird: Cactus Wren

The cactus wren, chosen as the state bird by the Arizona state legislature in 1931, is the largest wren in North America. Cactus wrens are insect eaters. They like to build their nests inside cholla or other cactus plants. The prickly cactus spines provide protection for the nest, which is lined with soft feathers.

ARIZONA

★ State Neckwear: Bolo Tie

The bolo tie was adopted as Arizona's official state neckwear in 1973. A silversmith from Wickenberg, Victor Cedarstaff, claims to have invented the tie in the 1940s. The bolo tie is a long leather cord that tightens around the neck with a sliding clasp.

★ State Gem: Turquoise

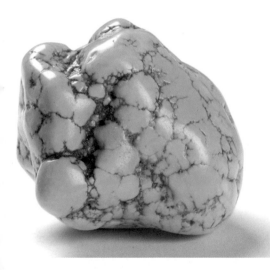

Turquoise is a blue-green gemstone that contains copper and aluminum. Many Native American groups of the Southwest use the gemstone in jewelry, crafts, and ceremonies. Long ago, the Native people of Arizona and New Mexico mined turquoise and carried the valued gem along the trade routes to Mexico.

★ State Amphibian: Arizona Tree Frog

In 1986, the Arizona tree frog was officially named the state amphibian, after Arizona schoolchildren voted for it in a poll. The small frog is green and brown and lives mainly in the forests of central Arizona's mountains. Arizona tree frogs can measure from three-quarters of an inch (2 centimeters) to 2 inches (5 cm) long.

The Colorado River meanders through Horseshoe Bend near Page, Arizona. The water is 1,000 feet (305 meters) below the viewing area on the cliffs above.

The Grand Canyon State

Arizona is a large state located in the southwestern United States. It is the sixth-largest US state, measuring 113,635 square miles (294,313 square kilometers) in land area. It has fifteen counties. The state is shaped almost like a square and measures approximately 400 miles (644 km) from north to south and 310 miles (499 km) from west to east. Arizona received its nickname, the Grand Canyon State, from the famous landform in the northwestern part of the state.

Arizona's landscape is commonly divided into three geographical regions: the Colorado Plateau in the north, the Arizona transition zone in the middle, and the Basin and Range region in the south. Generally, the state's higher elevations, ranging from 5,000 to 8,000 feet (1,525 to 2,440 meters), are in the north.

The Colorado Plateau

The Colorado Plateau is a traditional western landscape made up of plateaus: small plateaus called **mesas**, and even smaller plateaus called buttes. It is covered by ancient lava flows and cut by canyons. The canyons and buttes reveal layers of stone, minerals, ash, and fossils. The region's rivers helped create the canyons as they wore down the rocks over millions of years.

The rocks of the Grand Canyon appear to turn red at sunrise.

Arizona Borders

North:	Utah Nevada
South:	Mexico
East:	New Mexico
West:	California Nevada

The most famous of Arizona's canyons is located in the western part of the Colorado Plateau. The Grand Canyon is a popular destination for people from all over the world. The average depth of the canyon is about 1 mile (1.6 km), with the Colorado River flowing 5,000 feet (1,525 m) below the canyon's rim. Rainwater and snowmelt helped the Colorado River form the Grand Canyon, which is 18 miles (29 km) across at its widest point. The canyon is 277 miles (446 km) long and splinters into many side canyons. Although the world has larger and deeper canyons, the Grand Canyon is considered one of the most beautiful. US geologist John Wesley Powell explored the Grand Canyon and the Colorado River in 1869. He wrote about the immensity and grandeur of the canyon, describing it as "a broad, deep, flaring gorge of many colors." Scientists estimate that the oldest rocks in the canyon are close to two billion years old.

North of the Grand Canyon is an area called the Kaibab Plateau. The plateau is heavily forested with aspen, spruce, fir, and ponderosa pine. Animals including Kaibab squirrels, deer, turkeys, and bobcats make their home in the Kaibab Plateau.

South of the Grand Canyon, along the southern edge of the Colorado Plateau, is an area of 1,800 square miles (4,660 sq. km) filled with hundreds of dormant or extinct volcanoes. (Dormant volcanoes are not currently active, though it is possible they may erupt in the future. Extinct volcanoes are not currently active and are not expected to become active in the future.) This area, known as the San Francisco Volcanic Field, creates a scenic background for the city of Flagstaff. Most of the hills and mountains found between Flagstaff and the Grand Canyon are actually extinct volcanoes. The highest of these peaks is Humphreys Peak. It rises 12,633 feet (3,851 m) and is the highest point in Arizona. The state's youngest volcano, Sunset Crater, erupted sometime between 1040 and 1100 CE. It has been a national monument since 1930.

Erosion—the wearing away of land by wind and water over time—has shaped the eastern part of the Colorado Plateau. The strange shapes and rock formations of the badlands and the Painted Desert were carved by erosion. The wearing away of the land has also uncovered the mineral-filled logs of the Petrified Forest. In this forest, the wood petrified, or slowly changed into rocklike, mineral-rich material. The isolated buttes and mesas of Monument Valley in northeastern Arizona were also formed by erosion. The steep cliffs of the Mogollon Rim mark the southern boundary of the Colorado Plateau.

Volcanoes in the San Francisco Volcanic Field are either dormant or extinct.

ARIZONA
POPULATION BY COUNTY

County	Population	County	Population
Apache	71,518	Mohave	200,186
Cochise	131,346	Navajo	107,449
Coconino	134,421	Pima	980,263
Gila	53,597	Pinal	375,770
Graham	37,220	Santa Cruz	47,420
Greenlee	8,437	Yavapai	211,033
La Paz	20,489	Yuma	195,751
Maricopa	3,817,117		

Source: US Bureau of the Census, 2010

Thunderstorms regularly dampen the Twin Buttes in the summer. This beautiful rock formation is located near Sedona.

Arizona Transition Zone

Numerous mountain ranges fill the Arizona transition zone, located in a narrow strip of land across the middle of the state. The region is a transitional area between the higher elevations of the Colorado Plateau and the lower Basin and Range region. The area, sometimes called the "copper belt," is rich with deposits of copper-bearing minerals. The highest mountains in the transition zone are forested with Douglas fir and ponderosa pine trees. Pinyon pine and juniper grow at the lower elevations.

Arizona's largest city, Phoenix, is located in the center of the state. Many people come to central Arizona to visit this city. People also come to fish in the shady streams of the transition zone. During the winter months, many people ski and snowboard here. Loggers harvest the forests of the White Mountains in eastern Arizona. The state's second-highest mountain, Baldy Peak, is in the White Mountains. This peak, sometimes called Mount Baldy by Arizonans, rises to 11,420 feet (3,480 m).

Basin and Range

The Basin and Range region extends over southern Arizona. It is an expansive flatland with basins that are interrupted by abrupt, jagged mountains. The basins are shallow valleys that look like big, dry ponds. The effects of erosion mark this region too. The wind continues to carry away the soil and the fine sand from the dry, hard ground. The city of Tucson is located in this region, in the southern third of Arizona.

Erosion helped form the colorful landscape of the Painted Desert.

The massive Sonoran Desert occupies the southwestern part of Arizona. This desert has a total area of 120,000 square miles (311,000 sq. km) and extends west into California and south into Mexico. The Sonoran Desert is one of the hottest and driest deserts in North America. The hottest and driest sections of the desert surround the Colorado River. The tall, upright saguaro cactus, a common symbol for the state of Arizona, grows only in the Sonoran Desert. The desert is also home to small trees such as mesquite and ironwood, which provide some shade to the area. The creosote bush is the most common shrub in the driest lower elevations. Sprawling prickly pear, cholla cactus, and compact barrel cactus grow here too. Living among these plants are scorpions, reptiles such as rattlesnakes and Gila monsters, and various birds.

The saguaro cactus grows only in the Sonoran Desert.

Besides the Sonoran, Arizona also has parts of three other major deserts. The Mojave is located in the northwestern part of the state. Northeastern Arizona is home to the Great Basin Desert, and the Chihuahuan Desert is located in the state's southeastern corner.

Rivers

The waters of nearly all the rivers in Arizona eventually flow into the Colorado River. Among its tributaries—or smaller rivers that are connected to it—are the Little Colorado, the Bill Williams, and the Gila Rivers. The Gila is the second major river of Arizona, after the Colorado. It flows east to west across southern Arizona. The Salt River and the San Pedro River are tributaries of the Gila.

Dams across Arizona's major rivers form reservoirs and other artificial lakes. Water stored behind the dams is used to irrigate crops and to supply the needs of people living in urban areas. Hydroelectric plants at these dams generate

A Refreshing Sight

The town of Fountain Hills is home to one of the world's tallest man-made fountains. Built in 1970, the spray of the fountain can reach as high as 560 feet [170 m].

★ 10 KEY SITES ★ ★ ★ ★

Havasu Falls

Lowell Observatory

1. Cathedral Rock

Cathedral Rock is a large rock formation in Sedona, and is one of the most photographed places in Arizona. It is part of the Coconino National Forest. Cathedral Rock is a popular spot for hikers, who have carved steps into the rock's steep face.

2. Grand Canyon

About five million tourists visit the Grand Canyon every year, making it one of the most popular attractions in the world. In addition to sightseeing and taking photographs at the canyon's rim, visitors also enjoy hiking, rafting, running, and more.

3. Hoover Dam

The Hoover Dam opened to tourism in 1937. After the attacks of September 11, 2001, security concerns led to a new, modified tour that restricts access to most of the dam's interior. Still, nearly a million people visit the dam each year.

4. Lake Havasu

A large reservoir behind Parker Dam on the Colorado River, Lake Havasu is located on the border of Arizona and California. More than 750,000 people visit Lake Havasu every year to enjoy boating, fishing, and other activities.

5. Lowell Observatory

Lowell Observatory is a research facility in Flagstaff that is home to many powerful telescopes and other equipment for studying space and the stars. The observatory recently completed construction of the Discovery Channel Telescope, the fifth largest telescope in the continental United States.

ARIZONA ★ ★ ★ ★ ★

6. Mesa Arts Center

Arizona's largest art center includes four theaters, five art galleries, and fourteen art studios. In addition to art exhibitions and live performances by musicians, performers, and comedians, the Mesa Arts Center also offers art classes for students.

7. Mount Lemmon Ski Valley

Part of Coronado National Forest, Mount Lemmon is a popular spot for skiers and snowboarders. Winter isn't the only time of year to visit—take the ski lift up the mountain in the summer to see beautiful, forested landscapes.

8. Petrified Forest National Park

Petrified wood is the fossilized remains of trees or other vegetation from prehistoric times. This national park in northeastern Arizona is home to many pieces of petrified wood, plus fossils of plants, fish, and reptiles. The park is a popular site for hiking.

9. Pima Air and Space Museum

More than three hundred aircraft are on display at the Pima Air and Space Museum in Tucson, including planes from World War II and those used by NASA to launch space shuttles. The museum hosts educational activities for families.

10. Wupatki National Monument

This is an area rich in Native American **artifacts** and history. Visitors can view preserved pueblos—homes made from stone, mud, and other materials—built by the Anasazi and Sinagua people. Many were built atop mesas.

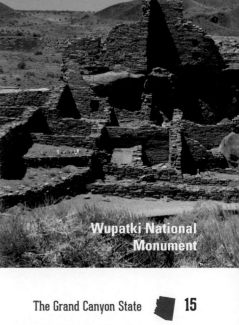

Pima Air and Space Museum

Wupatki National Monument

electricity using the power of the flowing water. The Hoover Dam, on the Arizona-Nevada border, was constructed on the Colorado River in the 1930s. It formed Lake Mead (located partly in Arizona and partly in Nevada), one of the largest artificial lakes in the world. The Theodore Roosevelt Dam was completed in 1911. This dam, built across the Salt River in south-central Arizona, helped to make Arizona an important agricultural region.

Climate

The wide range of landforms and elevations in Arizona creates extremes in the state's weather and climate. The southwestern corner of the state receives only 3 to 4 inches (8 to 10 cm) of rain each year—the least amount in the state. The state averages about 10 to 20 inches (25 to 50 cm) of precipitation each year. Many people think of Arizona as a desert, but the high mountains and Colorado Plateau can receive 10 feet (3 m) or more of snow every year. The melting of this snow helps to supply the state's main rivers.

Arizona has two rainy seasons. Gentle rains fall during the winter, between December and March, but Arizona receives most of its annual rainfall during the summer monsoon season, between July and September. During this time, summer storms can be quick and severe. A thunderstorm can pass through an area, hitting it with hailstones, sharp winds, and lightning. Rushing water soon floods the narrow canyons and the streets.

Monsoons occur in Arizona due to a combination of changes in weather. Changes in wind direction often happen during the summer. This change also brings an increase in

The Little Colorado River flows into the state's largest river, the Colorado.

Snow causes The Wave, an area located in the Coyote Buttes, to resemble a snowboarder's halfpipe.

moisture in the air. These shifts in weather patterns, combined with desert heat, help to produce storms that can include heavy rainfall and winds that cause dust storms.

Arizona also has a cycle of wet years followed by years of drought. During a drought, some areas receive no rainfall at all. Farmland dries out and cannot produce enough crops. Livestock and other animals also suffer from the lack of water. During times of drought, the danger of forest fires increases because the plants and trees are so dry.

Temperatures in the state also vary. Daytime temperatures in July can top 110 degrees Fahrenheit (43 degrees Celsius) in southern Arizona. The state's high plateaus average a more comfortable 90°F (32°C). In January, the temperature averages above 50°F (10°C) in southern Arizona. In the northern parts of the state and in the high mountains, temperatures can drop to below freezing after sunset.

Wildlife

Many animals, including coyotes, cottontails, bats, bobcats, squirrels, skunks, raccoons, foxes, and mule deer, live throughout Arizona. Small herds of antelope graze on the grasslands in the northern and southern parts of the state. Black bears, the only species of bear in Arizona, live in woodland areas. Peccaries—animals also called javelin or javelina, which resemble a small wild pig—roam among the cactus and mesquite. Mud turtles live in the ponds and rivers of the south-central part of the state.

In the desert, tortoises protect themselves from heat and cold by burrowing in the sand. Numerous snakes and lizards bask on the rocks or wait in the shade. The Gila monster, a large venomous lizard, lives in the desert.

A great variety of migrating birds stop in the Chiricahua Mountains of southeastern Arizona. Arizona is also known for its beautiful butterflies.

Endangered Species

Loss of or changes in natural habitat can cause animal and plant species to become endangered. This means their numbers have fallen so low that they are at risk of becoming extinct, or completely dying out.

In Their Own Words

"The wonders of the Grand Canyon cannot be adequately represented in symbols of speech, nor by speech itself. The resources of the graphic art are taxed beyond their powers in attempting to portray its features."

–John Wesley Powell, Explorer and Geologist

The building of cities and towns and the polluting of land and water most often affect natural habitats. The animals may not be able to find food or safe places to live. The plants may not thrive any longer. Some of Arizona's wildlife is in danger of disappearing, but many organizations and concerned residents are working together to try to help some of these endangered species.

The razorback sucker, or the humpback sucker, is a fish native to Arizona. It lives on the sandy bottom of rivers with strong currents. To spawn, or breed, it seeks quieter wetlands and backwaters. These fish used to live throughout the basins of the Gila and Colorado Rivers. Today, only a few hundred razorback suckers remain in the wild. The largest surviving population is found in Lake Mohave, behind Davis Dam on the Colorado River. Dams have changed the river currents and the sediments on the riverbeds. Dams also act as barriers and can prevent the razorbacks from migrating to their spawning areas.

To increase the number of razorback suckers, people are raising the fish in hatcheries. When the hatchery fish are old enough, they are released into the wild to live and breed with wild fish. Scientists are hopeful that the razorback sucker will survive. Although more than twelve million razorbacks have been released into the Colorado River basin, most have been eaten by nonnative fish.

A subspecies of gray wolf called the Mexican gray wolf is also endangered in Arizona. The wolves were once common in the central part of the state. By the 1900s, their numbers were greatly reduced by humans because of the threat they posed to livestock in the area. By the 1970s, the Mexican gray wolf had almost disappeared from the United States and Mexico. The US Fish & Wildlife Service listed this animal as an endangered species in 1976.

The population of the endangered Mexican gray wolf is slowing growing.

United States and Mexican wildlife agencies agreed to work together on a captive breeding program. In 1998, eleven wolves that had been raised in captivity were released into the Blue Range Wolf Recovery Area in eastern Arizona. Additional releases have followed. In 2002, for the first time since the release program began, a wild-born litter came from a wild-born parent. By 2010, it was estimated that the wild population numbered about sixty, and approximately three hundred additional wolves were being held in captive breeding facilities.

The Mexican spotted owl is listed as an endangered species in Arizona, in part because trees have been cut down where it lives. Additionally, the Mexican spotted owl has been affected by wildfires that destroy its habitat. In order to combat these issues and help increase the owl's population, Arizona officials are working to create protected areas where it can live. In these areas, it is illegal to cut down trees for commercial reasons. Special measures to prevent the start or spread of wildfires are also used in the protected areas.

Major Impact

The Barringer Meteorite Crater is considered one of the world's most well preserved craters. The crater was formed by the impact of a meteorite, a rock that hurtles through space and then enters Earth's atmosphere. Scientists believe the impact happened about fifty thousand years ago.

Black-chinned hummingbird

Gila monster

Mule Deer

1. Black-Chinned Hummingbird

Arizona's summer rainy season draws a variety of hummingbirds to the state. Many are migrating from the western United States to the tropical forests of Mexico and Central America. The black-chinned hummingbird is most common in open areas near Arizona sycamore and Fremont cottonwood trees.

2. Desert Anemone

Part of the buttercup family, the desert anemone is a flowering plant with white and pink petals. It thrives on rocky slopes and along the banks of streams. The flowers of the desert anemone bloom from February to April.

3. Gila Monster

Gila [HEE-luh] monsters are the largest land lizards in the United States. They can be as long as 2 feet (.6 m) and weigh as much as 5 pounds (2.3 kg). They have pink, orange, and yellow markings, and are named after Arizona's Gila River basin.

4. Mule Deer

The mule deer gets its name from its large ears, which resemble a mule's. These deer live throughout Arizona. They move to higher elevations during hot weather and lower areas in cooler weather. They feed on spring grasses, buds, and bark.

5. Ocotillo

The ocotillo bush is known for its spiny, whip-like branches that can grow as high as 20 feet (6.1 m). The ocotillo blooms every year and features red flowers that appear in the spring. It grows best in rocky, dry areas.

6. Pinyon Pine

The pinyon pine can be found in the northern forests of the high Colorado Plateau. Pinyon pines produce delicious, nutritious nuts that are a favorite food of both humans and animals. The wood of the tree has a distinctive scent.

Pinyon pine

7. Prairie Dog

Prairie dogs are small rodents with hairy tails and short legs. They are closely related to squirrels and chipmunks. Prairie dogs are known for a high-pitched call, similar to a dog's bark, which they use to communicate with other prairie dogs.

8. Rattlesnake

The dull colors of rattlesnakes help them blend into their surroundings. Eleven species of rattlesnake live in Arizona. Each snake has a rattle made of dried skin at the end of its tail and hollow fangs designed for injecting venom into its prey.

Teddy Bear Cholla

9. Teddy Bear Cholla

The teddy bear cholla gets its name from its spines, which make it appear soft and fuzzy from a distance. Its fuzzy-looking spines have tiny barbs that dig under the skin, making them difficult to remove. Teddy bear chollas grow throughout the Sonoran Desert.

10. White-Nosed Coati

This mammal, also referred to as a coatimundi, lives in the Sonoran and Chihuahuan deserts. Similar in appearance to a raccoon, it gets its name from the white fur at the tip of its snout. Coatis eat insects, fruits, small lizards, and mice.

White-nosed coati

 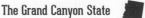

The White House Ruin in Canyon de Chelly is among the structures left behind by the Ancestral Pueblo people.

From the Beginning

People have been living in what today is Arizona for at least twelve thousand years. The first residents of present-day Arizona were the descendants of people who probably came to North America from Asia, crossing a land bridge that used to connect eastern Russia and Alaska. At their campsites, these early people left stone spear points called Clovis points. They hunted large grazing animals, such as mammoths and bison, which thrived on the region's grassy plains. By about 8000 BCE, the area's climate had warmed, and deserts replaced the grasslands. Most of the large animals died out.

People adjusted to these changes by hunting smaller animals, such as rabbits, and gathering nuts and berries. They eventually learned how to farm, which allowed them to settle in one place. They began to build houses of mud, stone, and wood. Many of the houses, now called pit houses, were built partially underground. Families built their houses close to each other and formed villages.

Over time, these first people developed distinct cultures in the deserts, mountains, and canyons of what is now Arizona. One of these groups used to be called Anasazi, which is a Navajo word meaning "enemies of our ancestors." Today, they are called Ancestral Pueblo people. They lived in what is now northeastern Arizona and northwestern New Mexico.

Casa Grande is the largest-known structure built by the Hohokam people of the Gila Valley.

King Copper

Copper has long been one of Arizona's most important resources, a fact that is celebrated in the copper roof of the state's capitol building. The amount of copper on the roof is enough to make more than 4.8 million pennies.

The Ancestral Pueblo people are the ancestors of the Zuni and Hopi people of Arizona and of the Pueblo people living in New Mexico. They built villages in protected areas on the sides of cliffs. Ruins of their villages can be found in Canyon de Chelly. The Ancestral Puebloans were part of a trade network that carried feathers, shells, salt, and turquoise to the peoples of the Southwest, Mexico, the Great Plains, and the Pacific Coast.

Another group of early Native Americans, the Hohokam people, lived in the southern part of present-day Arizona by the Gila and Salt Rivers. The Hohokams were expert farmers and grew many crops, including cotton, corn, and bean varieties. They built a large system of irrigation canals to bring water from the rivers to their fields. These canals have been discovered under the cities of Tucson and Phoenix.

The Hohokams built Casa Grande, a four-story structure between Phoenix and Tucson. The ruins of this building can be viewed at Casa Grande Ruins National Monument. Another group, the Sinagua people, built an elaborate cliff dwelling that can be seen at Montezuma Castle National Monument.

The Mogollon people lived in the desert mountain areas of southern Arizona and New Mexico. They farmed on the narrow ledges and moved often. Archaeologists have discovered distinctive pottery, often with black and white imagery. It is believed that the Mogollon people crafted these pieces.

Keet Seel, meaning "broken house" in Navajo, is one of three well-preserved cliff dwellings in the Navajo National Monument.

By the 1400s, the Ancestral Pueblo, Hohokam, and Mogollon people had left their traditional homelands. The Ancestral Puebloans moved to new regions in the late 1200s, while the Mogollon and Hohokam people moved sometime around the 1300s. Experts are not sure exactly why these native people left the area. Lack of rainfall may have made food scarce and life harsh, forcing them to move closer to water sources such as rivers. They may have been affected by disease. New people may have moved into the area and crowded them out. They may also have started living among the other cultures in the area.

Many Navajos and Apaches began moving into the area in about 1250 CE. The groups came from northern regions that include parts of present-day Canada and Alaska. At the time, the Navajos and Apaches belonged to one group. Sometime after moving to Arizona, they separated. The Navajos settled among the mesas of northeastern Arizona. The Apaches settled in the rugged mountains farther south.

The Native People

When you travel through parts of Arizona, you can still see the houses, art, and other evidence of the earliest people to call this area home. The first native people in this area were **nomadic hunters**, meaning they traveled in search of food. Over time, they began to settle in simple homes and turned to farming. The Ancestral Pueblo people, once known by the Navajo word Anasazi, lived in the northeastern part of the state. They built homes out of clay and stone, called pueblos, in the sides of cliffs and on top of plateaus. Several families could live in one cluster of pueblos. Around 600 CE, a group called the Sinagua began to make their homes in the central part of the state. Other groups that made Arizona their home include the Hopi, Yavapai, Apache, and Navajo tribes.

The customs and history of many tribes in Arizona are closely linked. The Sinagua and Ancestral Puebloan cultures followed similar patterns: their people traveled across the region hunting for food, and later lived in pueblos and farming. Historians believe the Hopi people are likely descendants of the Ancestral Puebloans and carried many of their traditions, including agriculture, forward. The Navajo who migrated to Arizona between 1000 and 1200 CE adopted many traditions of the Hopi while maintaining some aspects of their own culture and language.

When Arizona became a United States territory in 1863, settlers moving west drove many native people from their land. The Apache in particular faced conflict with US settlers. A famous chief named Geronimo led the Apache people during many of these battles. Although the Apache and Yavapai did not previously have much in common, they both battled with new settlers. They later lived in the same communities and reservations after they were driven from their homes in the late nineteenth century.

Over the years, many Native groups migrated to new areas or blended with other tribes to form Arizona's modern Native American community. Today the Navajo, Yavapai, Apache, and Hopi are officially recognized by the federal government. A federally recognized tribe is a Native American or Alaska Native tribal entity that is recognized as having a government-to-government relationship with the United States. These tribes are recognized as possessing certain inherent rights of self-government, such as tribal sovereignty. They are entitled to receive certain federal benefits, services, and protections because of their special relationship with the United States. At present, there are 566 federally recognized Native American and Alaska Native tribes and villages.

The Sinagua built what is now called Montezuma Castle National Monument.

Spotlight on the Hopi

The Hopi people have lived in Arizona for more than two thousand years. Many historians believe the Hopi moved to Arizona from southern areas such as Mexico and other parts of Central America.

Villages and Clans: The divisions in Hopi society were by the villages people lived in, as well as by clans within each village. The Hopi occupy twelve villages located in three regions: First Mesa, Second Mesa, and Third Mesa.

Homes: The Hopi people lived in pueblos, homes made of clay and stone. Pueblos usually have flat roofs and multiple levels. Entire extended families would live together in these pueblos. Often, the bottom level of the pueblo was an underground chamber, called a kiva, used for religious ceremonies.

Food: Farming was a very important part of life for the Hopi. Corn was the most common crop, and the Hopi grew more than twenty varieties of this vegetable. They also grew squash, pumpkins, beans, tobacco, and sunflowers.

Clothing: Because of the hot and dry climate, the Hopi wore simple clothing that would help them keep cool. Men usually wore a simple breechcloth and moccasins made of deer hide. Women often wore mantas, a light dress that went down to their knees.

Art: The Hopi made beaded necklaces and silver jewelry such as bracelets and rings. They are also known for their pottery and **intricately** woven rugs. When Hopi people took part in traditional ceremonies, they would paint their faces, with beautiful, complex designs.

Coronado led an expedition through Arizona in a failed attempt to find gold.

Spanish Rule

Spanish soldiers and missionaries—religious people who work to convert others to their religion—began traveling north from Mexico in the years after Spain conquered Mexico in 1521. The Spanish began to hear rumors of gold and other riches in cities farther north.

In 1540, Spanish explorer Francisco Vásquez de Coronado and a large party of men left Mexico City. They traveled north with a long line of horses, cattle, and sheep. The soldiers were looking for gold and hoping to claim territory and wealth for Spain. In fact, some thought the area that would become Arizona could be the location of the Seven Cities of Cibola—lands filled with gold and riches that were part of Spanish legend. They crossed the area that includes present-day Arizona and New Mexico and headed eastward into the Great Plains. The Spanish were disappointed. They did not find gold in the dry land and sometimes fought with the people native to the area.

In the decades after Coronado's exploration, most Europeans lost interest in the region that is now Arizona. Without the possibility of gold, they

Mail By Mule

The capital of the Havasupai Reservation, Supai, is an area so remote that you cannot access it by car. You can only reach Supai by helicopter, hiking, or riding a mule. Supai is the only place in the United States where mail is delivered by mule.

were not interested in settling an area where water could be scarce and the heat could be scorching. The area did hold interest for missionaries hoping to convert Native American groups to Christianity, however. Around 1629, Spanish soldiers supervised the building of missions all over Arizona and New Mexico. The missionaries forced the Native Americans to learn Spanish culture and practice Christianity instead of their own religion. In 1680, the Pueblo people in New Mexico rebelled and drove them out.

Jesuit priest Eusebio Francisco Kino is honored with a statue in the Wesley Bolin Memorial Plaza in Phoenix.

Missionaries were more successful in southern Arizona. In 1687, a priest named Eusebio Francisco Kino visited the Tohono O'odham (Papago) and Akimel O'odham (Pima) settlements in the Sonoran Desert. In addition to telling the native people about Christianity, he taught them European-style farming. He introduced wheat and grapes and brought sheep, horses, mules, and cattle. The people began to keep livestock. Father Kino was known for treating the Native Americans with kindness and respect. He eventually helped establish at least twenty-four missions in southern Arizona and northern Mexico.

Europeans were once again drawn to Arizona when a miner from the Yaqui tribe found chunks of silver near a farm called *Arissona* by the Spanish, located near present-day Nogales. Spaniards rushed from Mexico to dig up the ground and found more silver, but it soon ran out. Tensions grew between the Native Americans and the Europeans because the missionaries who followed Kino did not treat the Native Americans as respectfully as he had.

In 1751, the Akimel O'odhams revolted. They killed miners, settlers, and missionaries, and burned their houses and churches. To protect themselves from more attacks, the Spanish built a walled presidio, or fort, at Tubac in 1752. Soldiers stayed in the presidio and a town grew outside the adobe walls. In 1775, the Spanish government established a site for a new presidio at Tucson.

Making a Hopi Kachina Doll

The Hopi people make handcrafted figures called Kachina dolls. Each doll represents a different spirit, including the chief, a dancer, a hawk, the sun—any being the Hopi considered an important part of life. Make your own Hopi Kachina doll in a few simple steps.

What You Need

A cardboard tube from paper towels or
    toilet paper
Scissors
Tape
Glue
A small ball, clay, or other object for the doll's head

Paint, markers, or crayons
Brushes (if using paint)
Construction paper, felt, and/or fabric
Feathers, beads, buttons, and other
    decorative objects
A small, thick piece of cardboard

What You Do

- Cut two slits in the cardboard tube, opposite each other and about a third of the way up the tube. Make two short cuts at the end of each slit, making a T shape.

- Curve each flap you made with the cuts into tube shapes for the doll's legs.

- Use glue to attach the ball, clay, or other object to the top of the tube for the doll's head.

- Thinking of the theme you want your doll to represent, paint the doll's head and let it dry.

- Decorate your doll with clothes or designs using your construction paper, felt, markers and other objects.

- Make a base out of the thick cardboard, and glue your doll to the base. Color or decorate the base to represent the environment of your doll—for example, if your doll was a forest animal, you could decorate the base to look like the forest.

Mexican Rule

Just as Americans fought the American Revolution (1775–1783) to be free of British rule, people in Mexico wanted independence from Spain. Mexico began its struggle for independence in 1810. After eleven years of war, Mexico became an independent country in 1821. Present-day Arizona was now part of Mexico instead of Spain. After the war, there was little money left to help the settlers in the Arizona area. Instead, the Mexican government gave land grants in present-day Arizona to reward soldiers and leaders. Most of the land was used for cattle ranches. Some Spanish and Mexican land grants stayed with Arizona families for generations.

From 1846 to 1848, Mexico and the United States fought each other in the Mexican-American War. The war began after the United States claimed land that would become part of Texas. Mexico considered this land its territory. More than thirteen thousand American soldiers died in the war, though the vast majority died from disease as the result of unsanitary conditions. Records are incomplete for the number of Mexican soldiers who lost their lives, but some historians estimate around twenty-five thousand. The Treaty of Guadalupe Hidalgo, signed on February 2, 1848, ended the war. Under the treaty, a huge area of the Southwest was transferred from Mexico to the United States. This land included all of today's Arizona north of the Gila River and present-day California, Nevada, and Utah. Parts of present-day New Mexico, Colorado, Wyoming, Oklahoma, and Kansas were also included. However, the towns of Tucson and Tubac were still in Mexico.

The United States wanted more land from Mexico to build a southern-route railroad to California.

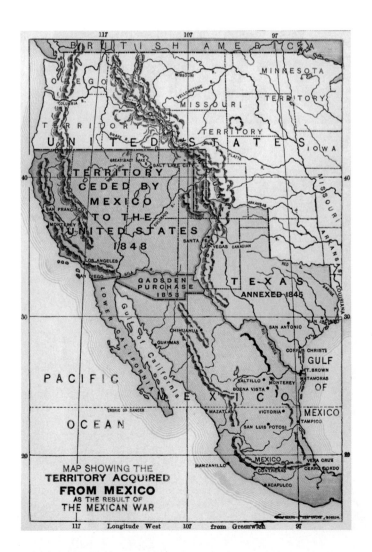

MAP SHOWING THE **TERRITORY ACQUIRED FROM MEXICO** AS THE RESULT OF THE MEXICAN WAR

Many hoped that this railroad would allow for expanded business and trade between the South and the Pacific Coast. In 1853, Mexico agreed, in what is known as the Gadsden Purchase, to sell to the United States a strip of land south of the Gila River in present-day southern Arizona and southwestern New Mexico. The treaty providing for this purchase was ratified by the US Senate the following year. Today's southern border of Arizona was set.

In the United States

Beginning in the late 1840s, Americans crossed Arizona on their way to the gold rush in California. Ferries at Yuma took them across the Colorado River. Others stayed in Arizona to search for silver and gold, or to raise cattle and grow wheat.

For a number of years, present-day Arizona remained part of the Territory of New Mexico, established by the US government after the Mexican-American War. In 1863, during the Civil War (1861–1865), President Abraham Lincoln signed the bill that created the separate Territory of Arizona. The new Arizona territorial government met at Prescott, the new capital. John Goodwin was the first governor of the territory.

Arizona had its own gold rush in the 1860s, when gold was discovered near La Paz, and later in Maricopa County. That mine, known as the Vulture Mine, was the source of more than 300,000 ounces of gold and 240,000 ounces from the time of its discovery through 1942. President Franklin D. Roosevelt closed the mine during World War II because

The Vulture Mine produced a lot of gold and silver before it was shut down during World War II.

industry was supposed to concentrate on the war effort. The rush associated with this discovery is credited with the founding of the town of Wickenburg.

Tensions between whites and Native Americans in the region increased. For years the Navajos and Apaches had fought against the Spanish and Mexicans. At first, the native peoples welcomed the American government and settlers. But misunderstandings and disagreements developed.

In an attempt to end the hostilities between the native tribes and the settlers, the US government established reservations in a policy to relocate the Native Americans. Some native groups agreed to go to reservations. Others did all they could to resist.

Moving the Native People

Christopher "Kit" Carson, a US army colonel, was sent by the US government to pursue the Navajos. He was told to gather some eight thousand Navajos and move them to Bosque Redondo, a barren camp at Fort Sumner in New Mexico. When the Navajo people resisted, Carson and his troops burned their crops and killed their livestock. Without food, the Navajos had no choice but to surrender.

In 1864, Carson forced the Navajos to travel to Bosque Redondo on what is now called the Long Walk. During this winter trek of 300 miles (480 km), thousands of Navajos died from exposure to harsh conditions. Navajos who survived the journey found life-threatening situations at the internment camp, including overcrowding, lack of clean water, and poor farming conditions. Those who did not die from smallpox or starvation at the camp were allowed to return to a reservation in Arizona after more than four years.

Geronimo led his people during the Apache Wars.

1. Phoenix: population 1,445,632

Arizona's largest city was settled in 1867 as a farming-based community. For many years, the "Five Cs"—cotton, cattle, citrus, climate, and copper—were the biggest drivers of Phoenix's economy. Many technology companies now call Phoenix home.

2. Tucson: population 520,116

Tucson is one of the oldest towns in the United States, established in 1775. In modern times the city has become a thriving artistic community with more than 215 art groups and thirty-five galleries.

3. Mesa: population 439,041

The earliest native people in Mesa, the Hohokam, built a large canal system that was considered extremely advanced for that time. The system helped them farm. Residents can still tour the Park of the Canals to view 4,500 feet of ancient canals.

4. Chandler: population 236,176

Chandler was founded by Dr. Alexander Chandler, the first veterinary surgeon in the territory of Arizona. For many years, farming, especially cotton, was the basis of Chandler's economy. Now, manufacturing and electronics are how many Chandler residents make a living.

5. Glendale: population 226,721

This city in Maricopa County is located just nine miles from downtown Phoenix. Glendale hosts a number of family-friendly cultural events each year, including the Glendale Chocolate Festival and the Glendale Jazz and Blues Festival. It is also known for its many antique stores.

Phoenix

Tucson

6. Scottsdale: population 217,385

Scottsdale has won many awards for being an enjoyable, safe place to live. During the twentieth century, a large number of artists moved to the city, including architect Frank Lloyd Wright. Today, Scottsdale's artistic community is thriving.

7. Gilbert: population 208,453

Gilbert was once known as the "hay shipping capital of the world." In recent years, the town has seen tremendous growth, increasing in population from 5,717 in 1980 to more than 233,000 in 2014. Most businesses in Gilbert focus on science and technology products or services.

8. Tempe: population 161,719

Before Arizona became a state, Tempe was made up of two smaller settlements: Hayden's Ferry and San Pablo. When they joined together, a settler named Darrell Duppa suggested the city be named after the Vale of Tempe in ancient Greece.

9. Peoria: population 154,065

Because of the region's dry, warm climate, the people of Peoria enjoy many outdoor recreational activities. Peoria has more than 25 miles (40 km) of hiking trails and thirty-three neighborhood parks that include fishing lakes, baseball fields, skate parks and dog parks.

10. Surprise: population 117,517

A woman named Flora Satler founded the town of Surprise in 1938. To honor her contributions and those of many other women who played a part in the town's history, residents established the Surprise Women's Heritage Trail in 2013.

Scottsdale

Tempe

The Apaches, who roamed a large area covering southern Arizona, New Mexico, and northern Mexico, also had conflicts with the US government. After the Civil War ended in 1865, American troops were able to concentrate on overpowering the Apache people in Arizona. Apache groups led by Cochise and Geronimo seemed impossible to catch. They knew their way in the mountains and often went to Mexico to escape the American troops.

Cochise, the Apache leader, never lost a battle but he grew tired of fighting. He surrendered in 1871, but escaped when he realized the US government planned to move his people to a reservation in New Mexico. He eventually agreed to go to a reservation in Arizona. Geronimo also moved to the reservation, but he and his followers left several times because of bad conditions. During his last escape, he and a small group of Apaches managed to avoid capture by the five thousand American troops pursuing them. This pursuit lasted for about a year. In 1886, Geronimo surrendered, ending the conflicts known as the Apache Wars. Smaller conflicts lasted into the twentieth century, including the Battle of Bear Valley in 1918 and an Apache raid on Arizona settlers in 1924.

Progress to Statehood

Despite these tensions, Arizona continued to grow and prosper. News of any silver or gold discoveries spread quickly. Young men began to move west, seeking their fortunes in the mining camps and towns. Miners collected all the ore they could find from streams, surface rocks, and shallow mines. Then, they hurried to the next silver or gold strike.

Some of the early Arizona boomtowns gained a reputation for being lawless. Tombstone was one of these boomtowns. Prospector Edward Lawrence Schieffelin found silver there in 1877. Tombstone grew rapidly into one of the biggest and most unruly towns of the West. One of the most famous shootouts in American history—the gunfight at the O.K. Corral—took place in Tombstone in 1881. Law enforcement officials, including Wyatt Earp and John Henry "Doc" Holliday, faced down a group of outlaws in a thirty-second showdown. Three men were killed in the gunfight. In 1887, an underground river flooded the silver mines, bringing the boom to an end.

Flight Tragedy

In the 1950s, airplanes sometimes detoured over the Grand Canyon so passengers could view the area. On June 30, 1956, two planes requested permission to fly over the canyon and collided. The Federal Aviation Administration, a government agency responsible for the safety of commercial airplanes, was created as a result.

Life for this farm family (photo circa 1890) and that of others in Arizona improved when the railroad arrived.

After President Andrew Johnson signed a bill in 1866 chartering a railroad to California, two railroad lines were built across Arizona in the 1880s. The Southern Pacific Railroad brought in Chinese laborers to lay the tracks of the southern route across the desert. The first passenger train reached Tucson on March 20, 1880, and the Southern Pacific's transcontinental route was completed in 1881. Two years later, the Atlantic & Pacific Railroad Company completed a rail line through Flagstaff and across northern Arizona. Next, short rail lines were added to connect other places to the main routes.

The arrival of the railroads changed Arizona. This slow-moving, remote territory was now connected to the western and eastern states. Before the railroads, the state's ranches and farms were usually small. Ranchers and farmers produced enough food for themselves and sold wheat and beef to the army forts and mining camps. Now, the large markets of California, the Midwest, and the East could be easily reached. Ranchers from Texas bought acres of Arizona grassland to create big cattle and sheep ranches. They loaded the animals onto trains bound for the stockyards of Kansas City, Missouri.

By 1890, copper had replaced silver as Arizona's most valuable mineral resource. Tons of rich copper ore were mined in Bisbee at the Copper Queen Mine, which opened in 1877. Phelps Dodge was the copper mining company that owned the Copper Queen Mine, though companies including Calumet and the Arizona Mining Company operated mines nearby. Although mining copper ore and refining the ore to extract the copper were expensive, there was a new need to fill. American cities and factories needed copper for electrical wires and machinery. The railroads made it possible to send copper ore from Arizona to the nation's industrial centers.

Earthshaking History

Though Arizona is generally at low risk for earthquakes, there are a number of faults—fractures in Earth's crust—in the northern part of the state. The first record of a damaging earthquake in Arizona's borders happened on January 25, 1906. The violent shock could be felt as far as Flagstaff.

Arizonans volunteered for Theodore Roosevelt's Rough Riders and fought in the Battle of San Juan in Cuba.

Although Arizona was not yet a state, it sent volunteer soldiers to fight in the Spanish-American War in 1898. Two troops of 250 men went to San Antonio, Texas, where they became part of the group called "Rough Riders" by then-Lieutenant Colonel Theodore Roosevelt, who would later become president.

Because Arizona was a territory, its residents could not vote for the US president. They had no voting representatives in Congress, but Congress could declare any territorial law invalid. The people of Arizona wanted their territory to become a state. Congress gave permission in 1910 for Arizona to write a state constitution. Congress and President William Howard Taft accepted the constitution, and Arizona became a state on February 14, 1912.

Unique Timekeeping

Arizona is one of only two US states that do not observe Daylight Saving Time (DST). Most parts of the state, except the Navajo Nation community, observe Mountain Standard Time. The Navajo Nation spans three states, so it follows DST.

Wars and the Depression

In 1917, the United States entered World War I (1914–1918). Many Arizonans joined the armed forces. Others stayed in the state, helping to produce the food and supplies that the troops needed.

Tensions grew between the owners of the copper mines in Bisbee and the miners. Miners worked under dangerous conditions for low pay. They tried to organize into labor unions and to demand better pay and working conditions. At the same time, the cost of copper was rising. The price rose from thirteen cents a pound at the beginning of World War I to thirty-seven cents a pound by March of 1917. On June 24, 1917, a union called the Industrial Workers of the World presented mining companies with a list of demands, including improvements to safety and working conditions. When mine owners refused their demands, a large number of Bisbee's miners went on strike. On July 12, 1917, the owners directed a large group of men to round up the miners. Any miner who would not quit the strike was shipped on a filthy train to a remote location in New Mexico and abandoned. In all, more than one thousand people were transported across the state line. The mining companies used guards to keep these people from returning. Many Americans were unhappy with the treatment of the miners and condemned the mine owners.

Beginning in 1929, hard times hit Arizona, along with the rest of the country. During the Great Depression, which continued through the 1930s, there was widespread unemployment and hardship. Eventually, Arizona began to redevelop its economy. Irrigation projects allowed agriculture to expand. The state benefited from the building of dams and highways and the resulting creation of jobs. Tourism grew, too. Word of the Grand Canyon's beauty had spread, and people wanted to see it for themselves. Arizona was also promoted as a healthful place to take a vacation or spend the winter. Health seekers came to the state, hoping that the dry climate would ease breathing problems and lung diseases such as asthma and tuberculosis.

After the United States entered World War II (1939–1945) in 1941, the US military used the open spaces of Arizona to train pilots. The state's clear skies and good weather made it a natural location for military air bases. One of these bases, Luke Field, was the largest fighter-training base for the Army Air Forces at the time, earning its nickname "Home of the Fighter Pilot." More than twelve thousand fighter pilots graduated from courses there during World War II. Factories produced aircraft, and the mines supplied minerals for defense companies. The military and the defense industries boosted Arizona's economy and led to significant population growth. In 1940, the population of Phoenix was sixty-five thousand. By 1960 it had become the largest city in the American southwest with a population of 439,000.

Growth and Balance

After the war, the military and defense industries stayed in Arizona. There was a boom in uranium mining in the late 1940s and early 1950s, in part to provide nuclear material for military uses. Motorola set up an electronics plant in Phoenix in 1948. Thousands of people moved to Arizona, and the economy boomed. Air conditioning units became widely available in the years after the war, allowing residents to live comfortably year-round. The state was a desirable place to relocate. Real estate developers built communities planned especially to appeal to retired people. Sun City, one of the world's first active retirement communities, opened west of Phoenix in 1960.

Ancient Peoples

Historians are still not sure what caused the end of the civilization of the Hohokam, one of the earliest groups of people in the area now known as Arizona. Some think drought drove them south into Mexico, while others think excessive salt on farm fields, flooding, or warfare could be the cause.

Sun City, one of the world's first active retirement communities, opened in 1960.

Over time, Arizona's growth began to deplete its natural resources. People have long recognized the importance of water to Arizona. Agriculture, manufacturing, and large cities have put a serious strain on the water supply. Arizona has two main sources of water. Surface water comes from rivers and the lakes formed by dams, while groundwater is pumped out from underground natural reservoirs. It has taken millions of years for the underground water to accumulate, and Arizona is taking out more groundwater than is being put in. Some places in Phoenix removed so much groundwater that big cracks opened in the earth.

Seven US states rely on the water of the Colorado River: Arizona, California, Colorado, Nevada, New Mexico, Wyoming, and Utah. Sharing this water has been a source of conflict between the states for decades. Arizona wanted to route its share to where the need was greatest.

In 1968, President Lyndon Johnson approved construction for the Central Arizona Project (CAP). This enormous water project was designed to bring Colorado River water to central and southern Arizona. The system of aqueducts, tunnels, and pumping stations

The Central Arizona Project (CAP) built the largest aqueduct system in the United States.

is 336 miles (541 km) long. It reaches from Lake Havasu, on the Arizona-California border, to the San Xavier Indian Reservation south of Tucson. After the US Department of the Interior Bureau of Reclamation had investigated the potential effects on the state's environment, construction began in 1973. In 1985, CAP water was first pumped to agricultural fields near Phoenix. CAP water came to Tucson in 1992.

Less groundwater is being removed from Arizona now that these systems are in place, but the amount is still too high. Arizonans are exploring ways to balance their water needs and water supply. Every April is "Water Awareness Month" in Arizona, when the state's Department of Water Resources encourages residents to try new ways of reducing water usage and waste. This is just one example of how Arizonans continue to adjust to the changing times and find ways to help the state progress.

10 KEY DATES IN STATE HISTORY

1. 1250

The Navajos and Apaches begin moving into present-day Arizona. Though their history in the state includes much conflict, both tribes maintain a presence in Arizona in present day.

2. 1540s

Francisco Vásquez de Coronado's expedition explores the region. His travels take him from Mexico through the southwestern United States to present-day Kansas.

3. 1752

Arizona's first European settlement is established at Tubac. The settlement's purpose is to protect Spanish settlers and missions in the valley of the Santa Cruz River.

4. December 30, 1853

With the Gadsden Purchase, the United States buys from Mexico today's southern Arizona for the purpose of building a transcontinental railroad.

5. February 14, 1912

Arizona becomes the forty-eighth state, the last of the contiguous—or connected by land—states to be admitted to the union.

6. February 19, 1942

President Franklin D. Roosevelt signs Executive Order 9066, allowing the military to send more than 110,000 Japanese-Americans to internment camps, including several in Arizona.

7. September 21, 1981

Arizonan Sandra Day O'Connor is confirmed by the Senate and becomes the first female US Supreme Court justice. She was nominated by President Ronald Reagan.

8. November 4, 2008

John McCain of Arizona loses the presidential election to Barack Obama. McCain continues to be a key figure in the US Senate.

9. January 8, 2011

Congresswoman Gabrielle Giffords is shot during an assassination attempt near Tucson. She survives, though thirteen others are injured and six die in the shooting.

10. June 30, 2013

Nineteen firefighters are killed while fighting an out-of-control wildfire, made worse by windy conditions, near Yarnell. The fire was ignited by lightning.

A weaver demonstrates how to make a traditional Navajo rug.

The People

For at least twelve thousand years, people have been moving into and through what is now Arizona. They have come looking for a good place to live, to farm, and to work. The federal government takes a census, which counts all the people living in the country, every ten years. According to the 2010 Census, 6,392,017 people lived in Arizona as of April 1 of that year.

Phoenix, with a population of 1,445,632, is Arizona's largest city. It is a part of Maricopa County. The second-largest city is Tucson, in Pima County, with 520,116 people. Other large cities are Mesa, Glendale, Scottsdale, Chandler, and Tempe. Arizona also has many towns. Some of these towns have only a few thousand or a few hundred residents.

The Faces of Arizona

Though Arizona is becoming more racially diverse, the state's population is still approximately 73 percent white. Most of Arizona's settlers were of European descent. They or their ancestors came from such countries as Spain, England, Ireland, France, Germany, or Italy.

For the most part, Arizona's racial minorities make up small percentages of the population. African Americans comprise just over 4 percent of the state's people. Arizona's population is only 2.8 percent Asian American. About 4.6 percent of the population is Native American.

About 30 percent of Arizona's people say they are of Hispanic or Latino origin. This means that they or their ancestors came from a Spanish-speaking nation or culture. Most Arizona Hispanics trace their roots to Mexico. Others have arrived from Guatemala, El Salvador, Colombia, Peru, and other countries in Central America, South America, and the Caribbean.

Native Americans

After California and Oklahoma, Arizona is the state with the most Native American residents. Many of these people are members of tribes that have lived in the same area for hundreds of years. Most of Arizona's Native Americans live on reservations.

The Navajo Nation is located largely in the northeast corner of Arizona (and also includes land in New Mexico and Utah). It is the largest Native American nation in the United States. It has the most members and the most land. The reservation has 180,462 residents and covers 27,673 square miles (71,673 sq km). The Tohono O'odham Nation is also large. Its land is divided into four areas in south-central Arizona. Other tribes with reservations in Arizona include the Hopi, Apache, Hualapai, Havasupai, and Yavapai people.

Arizona boasts the third-largest population of Native Americans in the United States.

The tribes govern themselves. They choose their own leaders, write their own laws, and run businesses. The Ak-Chin community and the Gila River community use their land for agriculture. The Navajo and Hopi Nations mine coal.

Native Communities and Celebrations

Many reservations in the state invite visitors to enjoy recreation spots and areas of natural beauty. Native American tribes in the state also run gaming casinos, which fund the building of houses, schools, health clinics, and community centers. The money from these casinos also helps pay for their police and fire departments.

Many Native Americans are dedicated to their communities and cultures. The Navajo Nation celebrates tradition with a seven-day festival held every year. Young people raised on Arizona's reservations blend modern American culture with traditional language and ceremonies. Many Native American nations fund educational opportunities. The Navajo Nation has a program devoted to college scholarships and financial assistance.

Native Americans also played an important role in supporting America's efforts in World War II. Philip Johnston grew up the son of a missionary on a Navajo reservation in Flagstaff. At the beginning of World War II, Johnston met with US Marine Corps officials. He suggested that military forces fighting against Japan in the Pacific use a communications code based on the Navajo language, a code that the Japanese would not be able to crack. At the time, fewer than thirty non-Navajo people—and no Japanese—knew the Navajo language. In May 1942, the military brought in twenty-nine Navajos to develop a code system. About four hundred Navajos served as "code talkers" during the war. They used telephones and radios to transmit classified information. The code was never broken.

Hispanic Americans

Arizona is home to nearly two million Hispanic Americans. The state used to be part of Mexico, and now Arizona and Mexico share a border. Spanish-speaking people have long been a large part of Arizona's culture. Spanish is widely spoken and read throughout the state. Many towns, mountains, and landmarks have Spanish names.

Navajo Necklace

The Navajo people are known for their stunning artwork and jewelry, the squash blossom necklace being one of their most loved designs. Made of silver, this necklace often has a crescent shape—a nod to the influence of Spanish settlers—and intricate beading.

10 KEY PEOPLE ★ ★ ★

Ira Hayes

Charles Mingus

Stephenie Meyer

1. Cesar Chavez

During his youth in Yuma, Cesar Chavez and his family faced many hardships. They later moved to California to work on farms. As an adult, Chavez co-founded the National Farm Workers Association to protect the rights and safety of farm laborers.

2. Sharlot Hall

At age eleven, Sharlot Hall fell from a horse while traveling through Arizona Territory and injured her spine. She wrote to distract herself from the pain. Hall collected oral histories from settlers, wrote poetry about the Southwest, and established a history museum.

3. Ira Hayes

A Marine corporal and Pima Native American from Sacaton, Hayes was one of six soldiers who helped raise the American flag during the Battle of Iwo Jima. This moment became one of the most memorable images of World War II.

4. Charles Mingus

Charles Mingus was born in Nogales in 1922. As a composer and bandleader, he reached for energetic rhythms, unexpected harmonies, and deep emotion. Mingus played alongside other famous musicians such as Miles Davis.

5. Stephenie Meyer

Stephenie Meyer, born in 1973, grew up in Phoenix. In 2003, Meyer had a dream about a human girl and a vampire. She turned the idea into the novel *Twilight*, beginning a best-selling series of books known as the Twilight Saga.

6. Stevie Nicks

This singer and songwriter was born in Phoenix and learned to perform as a child by singing duets with her grandfather. She found fame with her band Fleetwood Mac by writing and performing hit songs including "Landslide."

7. Sandra Day O'Connor

Sandra Day O'Connor spent much of her childhood near Duncan. She was an assistant attorney general, state senator, and judge. O'Connor made history in 1981 when she became the first woman to serve on the US Supreme Court.

Sandra Day O'Connor

8. Emma Stone

A native of Scottsdale, Emma Stone is an actress known for films including *The Help*, *Superbad*, and *The Amazing Spiderman*. She began her career at the Valley Youth Theater in Phoenix and made her debut in a performance of *The Wind in the Willows*.

Emma Stone

9. Kerri Strug

Kerri Strug, born in 1977 in Tucson, was the youngest US athlete at the 1992 Olympics. During the 1996 Olympics, Strug injured her ankle but continued to compete to help the US women's gymnastics team win its first gold medal ever.

10. Lewis Tewanima

Lewis Tewanima was born on the Hopi Reservation in Second Mesa in the late 1870s. Tewanima was a member of the US Olympic teams in 1908 and 1912. In 1912, he ran in the 10,000-meter race and won the silver medal.

Kerri Strug

Who Arizonans Are

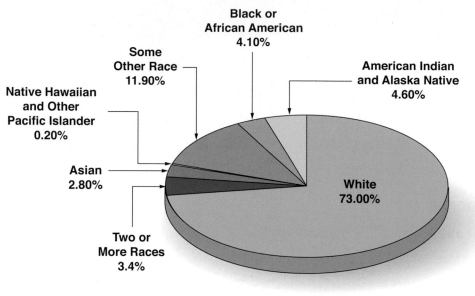

**Total Population
6,392,017**

Black or
African American
4.10%

Some
Other Race
11.90%

American Indian
and Alaska Native
4.60%

Native Hawaiian
and Other
Pacific Islander
0.20%

Asian
2.80%

White
73.00%

Two or
More Races
3.4%

Hispanic or Latino (of any race):
• **1,895,149 people (29.6%)**

Note: The pie chart shows the racial breakdown of the state's population based on the categories used by the U.S. Bureau of the Census. The Census Bureau reports information for Hispanics or Latinos separately, since they may be of any race. Percentages in the pie chart may not add to 100 because of rounding.

Source: U.S. Bureau
of the Census, 2010 Census

When the Southwest became part of the United States in 1848, many Mexican families lived there. They had farms and ranches along the Salt and Gila Rivers. They dug irrigation ditches to bring water to the fields and orchards where they grew wheat, hay, and fruit. The Mexican state of Sonora had many expert miners, who moved north to mine when they heard about the discovery of gold in Arizona. During the territorial period, more Mexicans settled in what is now southern Arizona. People from other parts of the United States came too, and many Mexicans sold their land to these new settlers and moved into towns.

In the 1880s, Tucson and Tempe had a majority of Mexican-American residents. Mexican Americans were civic and business leaders. They were active in politics, and many were elected to the territorial legislature.

In the 1900s, however, Mexican Americans often faced discrimination and poor treatment. Children had to attend separate schools. Mexican Americans struggled to find work and to earn fair wages. They joined labor unions to improve their work situation. The organization Alianza Hispano-Americana, formed in Tucson in 1894, joined forces with the National Association for the Advancement of Colored People (NAACP) in the 1950s. The groups campaigned for equal rights for citizens of Mexican descent.

In the 1960s, Mexican-American youths organized new groups throughout the Southwest. They demanded equal rights for Mexican Americans and encouraged Hispanic citizens to vote. Hispanic Americans have since regained an influential role in education, politics, and business in Arizona. The Hispanic population in Arizona is growing rapidly. According to some estimates, someday Hispanic Americans will make up a majority of the state's population.

Asian Americans

Chinese people began to arrive in Arizona in the 1850s. Like the other prospectors, they were looking for gold and silver. In the mines, they were paid low wages for dangerous work. In the towns and mining camps, they faced discrimination and abuse. In the 1870s and 1880s, railroad companies brought Chinese laborers to Arizona. These workers prepared rail beds and laid tracks for less than what white workers earned. After the mining boom ended and the railroads were completed, most Chinese left Arizona and returned to China. The few who stayed opened businesses or started farms.

Mexican Americans have long lived in Arizona.

Japanese immigrants came to Arizona in the late 1890s and early 1900s. They faced injustices and unfair treatment by people who resented the competition for jobs. The Arizona legislature passed laws restricting Asian marriage partners and residency, and the US Congress passed laws ending Chinese and Japanese immigration. The United States entered World War II after Japan attacked the Pearl Harbor naval base in Hawaii on December 7, 1941. In 1942, President Franklin D. Roosevelt signed an executive order requiring West Coast residents of Japanese descent to move to internment camps because of national security concerns. Arizona's Poston Relocation Center housed more than eighteen thousand Japanese-American detainees until its closing in 1945. Today, a memorial plaque there reads: "To all those men, women, and children who suffered countless hardships and indignities at the hands of a nation misguided by wartime hysteria, racial prejudice, and fear. May it serve as a constant reminder of our past."

Slowly, after the war ended, the treatment of Asian Americans began to improve. In 1946, voters elected Wing F. Ong to the state's House of Representatives. He was the first Chinese American to sit in any state legislature.

Today, more than 175,000 Asian Americans live in Arizona. They represent many nations, including China, Japan, India, Thailand, Cambodia, and Vietnam.

African Americans

Many African Americans came west in the 1800s, seeking a place to live and raise a family. They built homes and ranches, and worked at a variety of jobs. They prospected for gold and silver and worked for the railroads. Some African Americans were cowboys. Others started their own businesses, such as restaurants and barbershops.

African Americans did not have an easy life in Arizona during the early 1900s. School segregation, legalized in 1909, meant that African American children had to attend separate schools from white children. Most African Americans were restricted to living in certain neighborhoods. It was difficult for many black people to get a good education or a job that paid well. African Americans formed groups to oppose racial discrimination and unjust laws. They held demonstrations and sit-ins.

In 1951, the Tucson schools were desegregated, three years before the US Supreme Court prohibited legally segregated schools nationwide. In 1965, the state legislature passed a civil rights act, based on the federal Civil Rights Act of 1964, intended to end discrimination against African Americans in such areas as housing, voting rights, employment, and the right to go to restaurants, theaters, and other public places. African Americans began to be elected to local and state offices, and gradually life improved for them.

Arizona's Growth

Arizona has shown rapid population growth in each census since it became a state. From 2000 to 2010, Arizona's population grew by almost 25 percent. This made Arizona the second-fastest growing state, after Nevada, in that time period. Many experts expect that Arizona will continue to grow at a high rate.

Why do so many people move to Arizona? When business thrives in the state, Arizona appeals to job seekers. People are attracted by the promise of work and reasonably priced homes. They also enjoy the state's natural beauty and pleasant climate. Many people move to Arizona to be near family members. A growing number of retirees also move to Arizona to relax, play golf, or just settle into life in one of the state's many retirement communities. As the state's population continues to grow, it is clear that many people believe that Arizona has a lot to offer.

The US Department of Homeland Security estimates that Arizona is home to about half a million undocumented immigrants—people who have entered the country without permission from, and documents required by, the US government. In the late twentieth and early twenty-first centuries, many undocumented immigrants from Mexico and, to a lesser extent, from Central America have crossed the Mexico-Arizona border. They usually enter the country to seek better employment opportunities or to join family members. The US government has increased security measures along the border in an effort to prevent undocumented immigrants from entering the country.

In April 2010, Arizona governor Jan Brewer signed a law passed by the state legislature known as SB 1070. This state law required immigrants to carry their immigration documents at all times and gave police officers the authority to detain people suspected of being undocumented until their status can be verified. Some Arizonans, troubled by undocumented immigration, supported the law. Others, concerned that it could lead to discrimination against and harassment of Hispanic Americans in Arizona, opposed it. President Barack Obama argued that SB 1070 "threatens to undermine basic notions of fairness that we cherish as Americans." The federal government began a court case to overturn the law. Governor Brewer has said, "The law is constitutional, and we'll take it all the way to the Supreme Court if necessary."

Hispanics protested a bill targeting illegal immigrants in Arizona.

1. Arizona Renaissance Festival

More than 250,000 people attend this festival in Gold Canyon each spring to wear costumes, hear music, and enjoy dancing and performances—all in the style of the sixteenth century. Traditional food is served, and attendees can view and purchase crafts, jewelry, and other goods.

2. Bisbee 1000 Great Stair Climb

Bisbee is home to a system of public staircases that are the center of this fitness-friendly event. Participants run or walk through a 4.5-mile stair climb at a mile-high altitude. Musicians line the route and competitors wear costumes.

3. CFA Cat Show

Each December, Arizona's best cats compete in this Phoenix-based festival. Dozens of breeds are represented, and participants range from serious competitors to household pets. In addition to awards for the best participants, the event includes a cat costume contest.

4. El Tour de Tucson

Cyclists of all ages participate in this event that takes place in Tucson the weekend before Thanksgiving. The event appeals to riders of all ability levels, offering trails from hilly and challenging to flat and easy—all to raise funds for charity.

5. Lake Havasu City Striper Derby

Each May, this tournament brings Arizonans who love to fish to Lake Havasu. Participants are on the hunt for striped bass as they compete for more than $100,000 in prizes. Families enjoy the weekend's activities, which include a barbecue.

Bisbee 1000
Great Stair Climb

Lake Havasu
City Striper Derby

6. Scottsdale Culinary Festival

Nearly fifty thousand visitors attend this food festival each April in Scottsdale to sample gourmet food and drinks, see celebrity chefs, and enjoy events including a burger competition, a giant picnic, and chocolate tasting.

7. Tucson Festival of Books

Authors, exhibitors, and more than 100,000 attendees participate each May in one of the largest book festivals in the United States. The festivities include displays of fiction, nonfiction, children's, and many other kinds of books; a writing competition; and a workshop for writers.

8. World Championship Hoop Dance Contest

This event, hosted by the Heard Museum in Phoenix each February, showcases a unique Native American tradition using colorful hoops to create shapes and tell stories through movement and dance. Dancers are judged on their precision, rhythm, showmanship, creativity, and speed.

9. World's Oldest Rodeo

Established in 1888, this festival is also called Prescott Frontier Days. Held in Prescott, events include eight days of activities such as bronco and bull riding, steer wrestling, a parade, and a kiddie rodeo.

10. ZooLights at the Phoenix Zoo

Almost four million lights are part of six hundred light displays at this illuminating event, which has taken place each holiday season for more than twenty years. Displays include a life-size lion made of lights, a carousel, camel rides, and snow tubing.

Hoop Dance Contest

PRESCOTT · AZ

World's Oldest Rodeo

The 8-foot (2.4-meter) statue of the late
Senator Barry Goldwater greets visitors
at the Arizona State Capitol in Phoenix.
The statue was unveiled in 2014.

BARRY GOLDWATER
1909 - 1998

ARIZONA

How the Government Works

4

Arizona has several overlapping governments: federal, state, county, city, and tribal. The state follows the federal, or national, laws of the US government. But the state's own government also makes laws that Arizonans must follow.

The state is divided into fifteen counties. A board of supervisors chosen by popular vote leads each county. Counties are made up of cities and towns. Mayors and city councils head Arizona's cities and towns. County and city governments deal with local issues. Such issues include zoning decisions, city or town budgets, and public school matters.

Arizonans are represented in the US Congress in Washington, DC. Like all states, Arizona has two senators in the US Senate. The number of members each state has in the US House of Representatives is related to its population. After the 2010 Census, Arizona was entitled to nine representatives.

State Government

The state constitution went into effect when Arizona became a state in 1912. It is the basic law of Arizona. It guarantees the legal rights enjoyed by each person in the state. It describes how the state government is organized and what it does.

The Navajo Nation headquarters and a memorial to Navajo military veterans are located at Window Rock.

Like the federal government, the state government is divided into three branches: the legislative, the executive, and the judicial. Each branch has its own areas of responsibility, but they also work together. Officials of the state government meet and work in Phoenix, the state capital.

Arizona's territorial capital was established at Prescott in 1864. It was moved to Tucson in 1867 and back to Prescott in 1877. Phoenix became the capital in 1899, continuing as the capital through statehood in 1912 to the present day.

The Navajo Nation in Arizona is considered an independent government, with its own structure and leadership. Like the US government, the Navajo Nation is governed by three separate branches. The executive, legislative, and judicial branches work together to serve the Navajo people. A president and vice president lead the executive branch. Registered Navajo voters elect them every four years. The legislative branch is made up of the Navajo Nation Council and its Speaker. As of 2010, the Navajo Nation Council consisted of twenty-four delegates representing its 110 chapters, also elected every four years by registered Navajo voters. A district court and a supreme court form the judicial branch.

Branches of Government

Executive

The governor is the head of the executive branch. He or she is elected to a four-year term and cannot serve more than two terms consecutively. The executive branch also includes the secretary of state, state treasurer, attorney general, and superintendent of public education. With the other executive officers, the governor conducts the business of the state and enforces its laws. Doug Dacey became governor in 2015.

Legislative

The state legislature, which is called the general assembly, makes state laws. It is divided into two parts, or chambers: the Senate and the House of Representatives. The Senate has thirty members and the House of Representatives has sixty members. Each senator and representative is elected for a two-year term. He or she may serve no more than four consecutive terms. Senators and representatives write and vote on bills, or proposals for new laws. They also plan the state budget.

Judicial

The judicial branch includes the state's courts and judges. Every city has a municipal court. Every county has a justice of the peace court and a superior court. The state also has a Court of Appeals, in which people can argue the fairness of a previous lower-court decision. The Arizona Supreme Court is the highest court in the state. This court has five justices who are appointed by the governor to six-year terms. The Supreme Court creates the rules followed by all of the state's courts, judges, and attorneys. It hears appeals of lower-court decisions and can decide whether a state law violates any part of the state's constitution.

Citizen Lawmakers

In Arizona, private citizens are also lawmakers. Voters have the power of initiative, referendum, and recall at the state level as well as in their cities and counties.

In an initiative, voters propose a new law or an amendment to the state constitution. They collect signatures to have the initiative placed on the ballot. At election time, registered Arizona voters decide either for or against the new law or amendment.

In a referendum, people vote on whether a current law should remain in effect or proposed laws will go into effect. A referendum requires a petition signed by at least 5 percent of the state's voters. Any amendment to the state constitution must be put to a referendum. If people are unhappy with how an elected official is representing them, they may vote to recall, or remove, that official from office.

How a Bill Becomes a Law

Most state laws in Arizona are passed by the general assembly. Before a law is passed, it must go through certain steps. When an idea for a law is proposed, it is called a bill. Senators and representatives look for ideas for bills. Although citizens of the state often suggest these ideas, only elected legislators may officially introduce a bill. The bill is introduced to the Senate or the House. A bill introduced in the Senate travels first through the Senate, and a bill introduced in the House of Representatives travels first through the House.

After the bill is introduced, it is assigned to a committee for study. The committee may suggest ways to improve the bill. If the committee does not think the bill is worthwhile, it lets the bill "die" (that is, not move ahead to the next step). If the committee agrees with the proposal, the bill goes to the Legislative Council. The Legislative Council is a committee of senators, representatives, and staff attorneys. The council carefully studies the bill for any conflicts with existing law, including the state constitution. The Legislative Council then writes a draft of the bill in legal language.

At this point, the bill is formally presented to the Senate or House of Representatives. The title of the bill is read aloud, and the bill is assigned a number. The day after a bill is

Arizonans line up to cast their ballots.

The Arizona State Capitol is located in Phoenix.

first read, it is eligible for a second reading. In the Senate, bills are assigned to a committee after the second reading.

This committee again examines the bill and discusses the benefits and effects of the bill. The committee often holds public hearings. Citizens, organizations, and businesses may speak before the committee and explain how they believe the bill could be helpful or harmful. If the committee decides that the bill requires changes, it adds amendments to the bill. The committee then votes on whether to recommend the bill to the house or senate. If the bill has passed the committee and made it to the Senate or the House, the legislators debate the bill. Eventually, they vote on whether or not to approve the bill. When the bill is approved, it goes to the other legislative house and the process repeats. If the two houses pass different versions of the bill, a conference committee meets to resolve the differences. Then the two houses vote again to approve the final version.

Once the bill has passed in both the Senate and the House of Representatives in exactly the same form, it goes to the governor. If he or she approves of and signs the bill, it becomes a law. Sometimes the governor does not support a bill. He or she can then veto, or reject, the bill. If that happens, the legislators can vote again on the bill. If two-thirds of the members of each chamber approve the bill, then they have succeeded in overriding the governor's veto. The bill becomes a law even without the governor's signature.

POLITICAL FIGURES
FROM ARIZONA

Gabrielle Giffords, US Congresswoman, 2007-2012

Gabrielle Giffords represented Arizona's eighth district in the US House of Representatives. On January 8, 2011, Giffords survived an assassination attempt when a gunman opened fire at a public event. She later resigned from office due to her injuries.

John McCain, US Senator, 1987-

John McCain has been a key figure in Arizona and national politics since the early 1980s. Before that, he served in the US Navy and was a prisoner of war in Vietnam. His career has included time as a congressman, senator, and presidential candidate.

Janet Napolitano, Secretary of Homeland Security, 2009-2013

Janet Napolitano previously served as attorney general and governor of Arizona. She was the United States Secretary of Homeland Security during President Barack Obama's first term. In this role, she oversaw the government institutions that are in charge of keeping the United States safe.

Contacting Lawmakers

If you are interested in learning more about Arizona's legislators, visit: **www.azleg.gov/alisStaticPages/HowToContactMember.asp**

On this website you will find information about current legislation. By clicking on where you live on the interactive map, you can find your state representative and senator, along with their email addresses and phone numbers.

Former Arizona governor Jan Brewer.

Battle Over Voting

In 2013, the Arizona legislature passed a law approving changes to the state's election laws. Republicans favored the approved bill, but it angered voter-rights groups. The law changed many ways in which elections are run. One was to put more restrictions on voter initiatives. A second made it harder for third-party candidates to get on the ballot. Another was to drop people from the early voting list if they had not voted in two consecutive primary and general elections. People on the early voting list receive a ballot that is mailed to them about twenty-six days before an election.

Citizens groups and labor unions started petition drives to delay the bill from taking effect. They wanted the delay so that people could vote on the bill in a referendum. They gathered more than 146,000 signatures. The protest against the bill was so strong that Republicans in the legislature decided to pass a new bill that got rid of the new election laws. In doing so they explained they were just "listening to their **constituents**."

Despite the objections of those who wanted the people to vote on the election laws in a referendum in November 2014, the legislature passed House Bill 2196 in February 2014, and then Arizona Governor Jan Brewer signed the bill into law. Therefore, there was no longer a need for the referendum.

Solar power companies employ
thousands of Arizo...

5

Making a Living

The people of Arizona are skillful and resourceful when it comes to making a living. Many work in the traditional careers of farming, mining, or raising livestock. Many have tried new technologies and markets for their services and products.

Agriculture

Irrigation has made Arizona into an important agricultural state. Without it, much of the state's land would be too dry for farming. The state enjoys favorable weather with abundant sunshine and a nearly year-round growing season. The land of southern Arizona along the Gila River and in the west along the Colorado River is filled with huge fields of vegetables, citrus fruits, and cotton. Many leafy green crops such as lettuce do especially well in the mild winters of the low desert.

Agriculture brings in a little more than $9 billion to the state. The biggest revenue-producing crops in Arizona are lettuce, hay, and cotton. The state grows enough cotton each year to make a pair of jeans for every person in the United States.

The state's farms also grow broccoli, cauliflower, cantaloupe, and honeydew melons. Citrus groves produce lemons, grapefruits, oranges, and tangerines. The fruit is sold fresh or processed for frozen juice concentrate and other products. Arizona also grows carrots, potatoes, spinach, onions, parsley, and the Chinese cabbage called bok choy.

A farmworker pumps water to irrigate fields in Yuma.

Arizona's lands are also used to raise livestock. Ranchers keep alive the Old West tradition of breeding cattle, sheep, and goats. Arizona's grasslands are ideal places for herds of cattle and sheep to graze. The Navajos raise Angora goats, known for their soft mohair.

Minerals and Other Resources

Arizona's ancient volcanoes have left the land rich with valuable minerals. Lush forests that grew when the climate was wetter have been transformed into coal beds and pockets of oil and natural gas.

Arizona's first industry—mining—is still important to the state. Today's miners collect copper, molybdenum, silver, **gemstones**, and sand and gravel from the earth. Freeport-McMoRan Copper & Gold owns an open-pit mine north of Morenci. The mine is Morenci's biggest employer and the largest copper-producing site in North America. Copper ore is the most plentiful and valuable mineral found in Arizona. Copper has many uses, especially in electronics. Molybdenum is used as a lubricant and in steel alloys.

Arizona has other natural resources above the ground. The high mountains of eastern Arizona support many acres of pine forests. These forests are harvested for timber. Arizona's waterways are also an important resource. The state's dams store vital water supplies, which are being reduced by a lengthy drought. Hydroelectric plants built alongside the dams generate electricity for Arizonans.

More copper is produced at the open-pit mine near Morenci than at any other site in the United States.

Solar energy use is becoming more common in Arizona, as more people turn to renewable energy sources. In addition to helping the environment, this movement toward renewable energy is helping the state's economy by creating new jobs. Six renewable energy companies moved to Phoenix in 2010, including Power-One Inc., the largest US manufacturer of renewable energy conversion devices. Among other products, Power-One creates devices that produce electricity using solar panels.

Manufacturing

Arizona is a center for research and manufacturing of semiconductors. These electronic components are essential to computers, communications networks, and many electronic devices. The Intel Corporation, the world's largest semiconductor chipmaker, has a large office complex in Chandler. The company employs nearly ten thousand Arizonans.

The plastics industry in Arizona is growing to meet the demand for plastic products. Manufacturers use molds to shape plastic into lightweight, strong cases for cell phones, pagers, laptop and desktop computers, electronic organizers, and other electronic devices. Arizona's plastics industry also makes disposable medical supplies and parts and coatings for airplanes and missiles.

The aerospace industry came to Arizona during World War II. Aircraft companies today make engines and controls for military, commercial, and private jets. They also develop missile systems for the military.

★ 10 ★ KEY INDUSTRIES ★

Aerospace and Defense

1. Aerospace and Defense

Arizona's dry climate, abundant clear skies, and many respected research universities make it an ideal location for studying space and defense technologies. The state is home to more than 1,200 aerospace and defense companies.

2. Citrus

Arizona's warm climate and well-drained soil make it one of just four states that can commercially grow citrus. Arizona is second only to California in lemon production, and continues to be one of the largest producers of oranges and grapefruit in the United States.

3. Copper

Copper is a core component of Arizona business, thanks to vast underground reserves of the mineral. Arizona has been the leading copper producer in the United States since the late 1800s. In 2011, copper mining had a $4.6 billion impact on the state's economy.

4. Farming

Farming has been a part of Arizona culture since the region's earliest people built irrigation systems to water to their crops. Today, there are approximately 7,500 farms in Arizona producing cotton, lettuce, apples, and dairy products.

5. Government

The state government is Arizona's largest employer. About 70 percent of the land in Arizona is government owned, and many Arizonans work to support these areas, including in its national parks, tourist regions, or utility resources.

Citrus

6. Manufacturing

Large amounts of computer and electronic equipment, such as microchips, are manufactured in Arizona. Metal products, food products such as soft drinks or animal feed, and chemicals are also key parts of the manufacturing industry.

7. Mining

Arizona is known best for copper, but many other minerals are mined in the state. Gold, zinc, and silver can also be found within Arizona's earth, as well as uranium, manganese, and tungsten. Construction sand and gravel are mined as well.

8. Ranching

Another of Arizona's core industries is cattle ranching. People have been raising cattle in Arizona for more than three hundred years. Arizona ranchers produced enough beef in 2010 to feed 4.6 million Americans.

9. Science and Technology

Biotechnology, the study of life-based sciences for technological or business purposes, is a booming industry in Arizona. Many of these companies design or make products that help treat diseases or ailments, improve the way we use energy resources, or solve other problems.

10. Tourism

Tourists visit Arizona throughout the year to enjoy the state's warm and dry weather, historical landmarks, and natural beauty. Tourism-related businesses, such as hotels, restaurants, and travel agencies, all benefit from Arizona's popularity as a vacation spot.

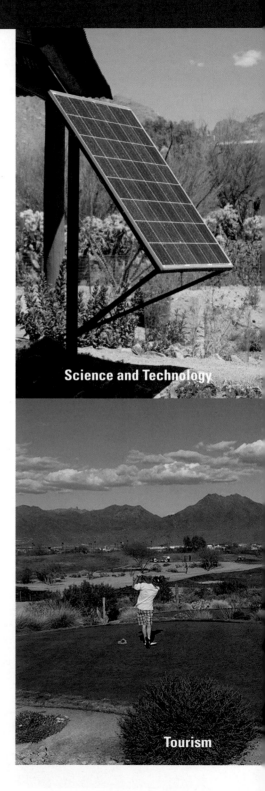

Science and Technology

Tourism

Recipe for Black Bean and Corn Salad

Arizonans enjoy many foods that reflect their cultural background and history, especially Mexican cuisine. This salad is healthy and easy to make. It also features many ingredients grown and enjoyed in Arizona and often featured in Mexican food—corn, cilantro, black beans, limes, and more. This recipe makes a great side dish for dinner, or a light lunch. Be sure to have an adult help you with the chopping and slicing.

What You Need

2 15-ounce (887-milliliter) cans of black beans, drained

1½ cups (355 mL) frozen or canned corn kernels (drain if using canned)

1 diced avocado

1 chopped red bell pepper

2 chopped tomatoes

6 thinly sliced green onions

1/2 cup (118 mL) chopped fresh cilantro

1/3 cup (78 mL) lime juice

1/4 cup (59 mL) olive oil

1 minced clove garlic

1 teaspoon (4.9 mL) salt

1/8 teaspoon (.6 mL) cayenne pepper

What To Do

- Combine lime juice, olive oil, garlic, salt, and cayenne pepper in a small container or bowl.
- Cover and shake until all ingredients are well mixed.
- In a large salad bowl, combine beans, corn, avocado, pepper, tomatoes, onion, and cilantro.
- Pour lime dressing over the salad.
- Mix well to combine, and serve. Enjoy!

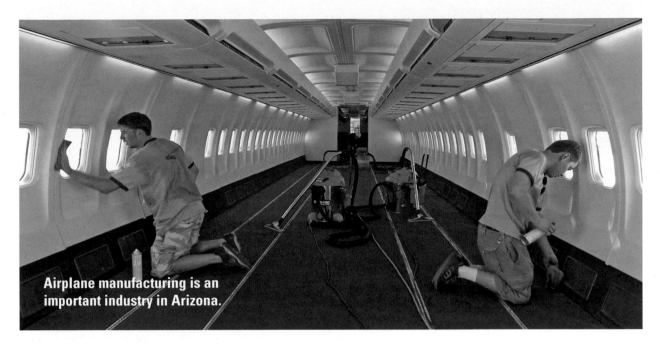

Airplane manufacturing is an important industry in Arizona.

Products and Resources

Lemons

Spanish missionaries planted lemons in Arizona. Growers now produce a variety of lemons in sunny, irrigated groves. Most of the state's lemons are grown in Yuma County. Lemons from Arizona are sold throughout the world.

Construction

Construction workers build new neighborhoods for the many people moving to Arizona. They build houses, schools, stores, industrial parks, civic centers, and stadiums. Arizona's construction industry has slowed in recent years as the number of new homes being built has decreased. Many Arizonans are still employed by the industry, however.

Semiconductors

Several companies that manufacture semiconductors are located in Arizona. Semiconductors can conduct electricity at high temperatures. They are used in computers, video games, wireless phones, and many other electronics products.

Copper

Arizona produces more copper than any other state in the United States. The Morenci Mine in southeastern Arizona is the largest copper mine in the country. It produces more than 800 million pounds (360 million kilograms) of copper per year. Arizona copper is used in electrical wiring, jewelry, and all kinds of appliances and electronics products.

Tourism

Arizona's natural beauty and Native American culture attract many visitors. Especially in the winter months, tourists visit Arizona resorts to relax and play golf. The many lakes attract people who like to boat and fish.

Aerospace

Aerospace companies in Arizona design and build jet airplanes and missiles. They also supply many of the parts that go into constructing aircraft. Some companies build the black boxes that record the details of an airplane's flight.

Science and Technology

Astronomers come to Arizona to study the sun, the stars, and the planets. The dry air and the elevation, where there is less light pollution, are ideal for observing objects in space. Some telescopes use mirrors and lenses to collect visible light. Other telescopes detect radio signals and microwaves.

Several telescopes make up the Kitt Peak National Observatory in the mountains west of Tucson. The Smithsonian Institution operates the Fred Lawrence Whipple Observatory on Mount Hopkins, south of Tucson. Another collection of telescopes is stationed at the Mount Graham International Observatory, near Safford. The US Naval Observatory in the mountains of Flagstaff uses instruments and measurements to provide the official time for the US Department of Defense. The Lowell Observatory, also at Flagstaff, is one of the oldest observatories in the country. Established in 1894, it was named a National Historic Landmark in 1965.

Arizona is known for its **biotechnology** industry. Biotechnology uses the molecular ingredients of living things to develop new products, such as medicines. Biotechnology brings together the skills and knowledge of many scientific specialists. Today, Arizona is home to more than seventy biotech companies, located mostly in the southern part of the state.

Transportation and Trade

Arizona is a transportation hub. Highways cross the state and domestic and international flights land at the airports in Phoenix, Tucson, and Yuma.

Arizona is located at a crossroads between the United States and Mexico. Long before the arrival of Europeans, the people living in Arizona carried on trade with the people living to the south in Mexico. The Arizona-Mexico Commission (AMC) was established in

1959. This nonprofit group works to improve trade relations and help with issues relating to the shared border. Since the North American Free Trade Agreement (NAFTA), which went into effect in 1994, removed barriers to trade between the United States, Mexico, and Canada, Arizona's foreign trade activity has increased. Many of the goods traveling between Mexico and the United States pass through Tucson.

Services

Food markets and retail stores are among Arizona's largest employers. Tourism is another important part of the service industry. The tourism industry includes airports, restaurants, hotels and resorts, companies that provide organized tours, and companies that rent cars and boats.

Arizona has a wide range of natural, historical, and recreational sites. Visitors enjoy outdoor activities such as bicycling, hiking, hunting, fishing, and boating. They travel to archaeological sites and places that are reminders of the Old West.

Professional sports are another big part of Arizona's tourism industry. Major League Baseball fans can root for the Arizona Diamondbacks. During football season, fans cheer on the National Football League's Arizona Cardinals. The state is also home to two professional basketball teams: the Phoenix Suns of the National Basketball Association and the Phoenix Mercury of the Women's National Basketball Association. Despite its climate, Arizona even has a team in the National Hockey League—the Arizona Coyotes.

Many people in Arizona work in city, county, or state government. Many Arizonans find jobs at the state's colleges and universities, including Arizona State University, Northern Arizona University, and the University of Arizona. Some Arizonans work as police officers or park rangers.

The US military is a major employer in Arizona. The Air Force, Army, and Marine Corps have bases in Arizona where pilots and soldiers are stationed and trained. Many civilian, or nonmilitary, employees and suppliers are employed at the bases.

Arizona relies on its growing industries and its hardworking residents. Working together and adjusting to today's economic challenges, Arizonans continue to strive to make their state successful.

> ### In Their Own Words
>
> "Imagination is as vital to any advance in science as learning and precision are essential for starting points."
>
> —Percival Lowell, founder of Lowell Observatory

★ARIZONA
STATE MAP

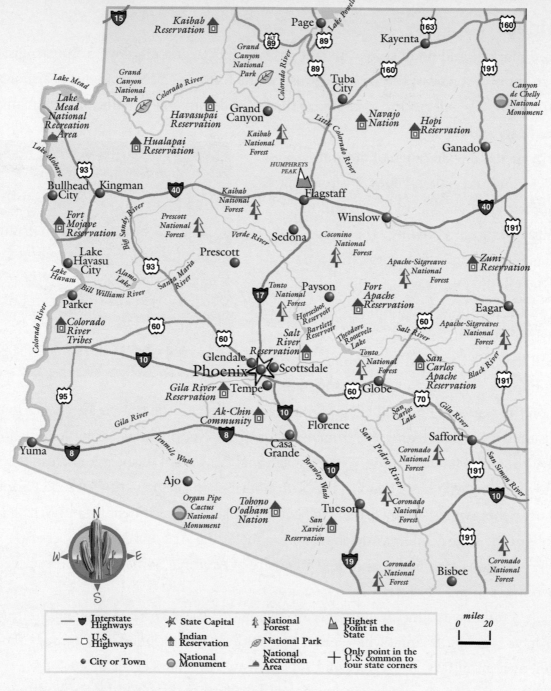

Kaibab Reservation

Page

Lake Powell

Kayenta

15

ALT 89

163

160

89

Grand Canyon National Park

89

Tuba City

160

191

Grand Canyon National Park

Colorado River

Navajo Nation

Hopi Reservation

Canyon de Chelly National Monument

Lake Mead

Lake Mead National Recreation Area

Havasupai Reservation

Grand Canyon

Colorado River

Little Colorado River

Ganado

Lake Mohave

Hualapai Reservation

Kaibab National Forest

93

Bullhead City

Kingman

40

Kaibab National Forest

HUMPHREYS PEAK

Flagstaff

Winslow

40

Fort Mojave Reservation

Big Sandy River

Prescott National Forest

Verde River

Sedona

Coconino National Forest

Apache-Sitgreaves National Forest

Zuni Reservation

191

Lake Havasu City

Lake Havasu

Alamo Lake

93

Santa Maria River

Prescott

Tonto National Forest

Payson

Fort Apache Reservation

Eagar

60

Apache-Sitgreaves National Forest

191

Parker

Bill Williams River

17

Horseshoe Reservoir

Colorado River

Colorado River Tribes

60

60

Salt River Reservation

Bartlett Reservoir

Theodore Roosevelt Lake

Salt River

Tonto National Forest

San Carlos Apache Reservation

Black River

10

Glendale

Phoenix

Scottsdale

60

Globe

70

191

95

Gila River Reservation

Tempe

San Carlos Lake

Gila River

Ak-Chin Community

10

Florence

Safford

Yuma

8

Gila River

Tenmile Wash

Casa Grande

8

Brawley Wash

10

San Pedro River

Coronado National Forest

191

San Simon River

10

Ajo

Organ Pipe Cactus National Monument

Tohono O'odham Nation

Tucson

Coronado National Forest

San Xavier Reservation

191

19

Coronado National Forest

Bisbee

Coronado National Forest

N

W   E

S

miles

0   20

— 🛡 Interstate Highways

⬢ U.S. Highways

● City or Town

✸ State Capital

🏛 Indian Reservation

🔵 National Monument

🌲 National Forest

🍃 National Park

🔺 National Recreation Area

🔺 Highest Point in the State

+ Only point in the U.S. common to four state corners

ARIZONA
MAP SKILLS

1. How many Native American reservations are listed on the map?

2. Which national park would you visit first if you traveled east from Havasupai Reservation?

3. Name a highway that intersects with Arizona's state capital.

4. What is the closest city located north of Parker?

5. If you traveled north on Route 191 from Eagar, which reservation would you reach first?

6. What city shown on this map is located at the most southern point?

7. What city is located approximately 20 miles (32 km) southwest of Flagstaff?

8. Which interstate travels the shortest distance in the state?

9. If you were in Tuba City and wanted to drive to Kayenta, which main route should you take?

9. Which direction should you go to travel from Ajo to Winslow?

Grand Canyon National Park

Bisbee

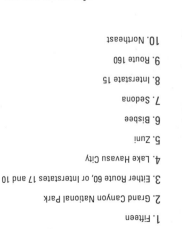

1. Fifteen
2. Grand Canyon National Park
3. Either Route 60, or Interstates 17 and 10
4. Lake Havasu City
5. Zuni
6. Bisbee
7. Sedona
8. Interstate 15
9. Route 160
10. Northeast

State Flag, Seal, and Song

The colors of the flag of Arizona recall the history of the state. The red and yellow rays in the upper half of the flag represent the red and yellow flags carried by Spanish explorers. The blue of its lower half matches the blue of the US flag. The copper-colored star in the middle commemorates Arizona as the largest producer of copper in the nation. Thirteen red and yellow rays represent the thirteen original colonies of the United States and are designed as a likeness of the setting sun. The flag, designed by Colonel Charles W. Harris, was adopted in 1917.

Arizona's state seal is in the shape of a shield. It shows the sun rising between the mountains. On the right side, there is a dam, a reservoir, irrigated fields, and cattle. To the left, a miner stands in front of a quartz mill. The motto at the top reads *Ditat Deus*, Latin for "God enriches." A circular band bearing the words "Great Seal of the State of Arizona" surrounds the seal. Printed along the bottom is the year that Arizona became a state: 1912.

The state song, "Arizona March Song," was written by Margaret Rowe Clifford and set to music by Maurice Blumenthal. It was adopted by the Fourth Arizona State Legislature on February 28, 1919. The lyrics can be found at www.50states.com/songs/arizona.htm.

Glossary

artifacts Objects made by people in the past that provide clues to their ways of life.

biotechnology The study of life-based sciences for use in technology and business.

constituents The people who live in a region represented by a politician.

contiguous Touching along boundaries often for considerable distances. Arizona was the last of the contiguous states to be admitted to the Union.

delegates People sent, elected, or authorized to represent others in their community.

gemstone A stone that can be cut and polished, and used in jewelry.

intricate Very complicated or detailed; often used to describe works of art, design, or jewelry.

mesa An elevated area of land with a flat top and sides that are usually steep. The word "mesa" is Spanish for "table."

meteorite A meteor that survives traveling through Earth's atmosphere and strikes the ground.

nomadic hunters People who roam from place to place to follow animals for food.

petrified wood Fossilized remains of trees or tree-like plants, usually from prehistoric times.

pueblo A settlement or apartment-like structure built by Native Americans in the southwestern United States.

referendum A vote by citizens on a specific topic or question that has been referred to them for a decision.

sit-in A form of protest in which demonstrators refuse to leave a certain place until their demands are met.

More About Arizona

BOOKS

Dwyer, Helen. *Hopi History and Culture*. New York: Gareth Stevens Publishing, 2011.

Jacobs, Bonnie Apperson, and Terri Manwaring. *Arizona Agriculture: Bee's Amazing Adventure*. Chandler, AZ: Little Five Star Publishing, 2014.

Mann, Elizabeth. *The Hoover Dam: The Story of Hard Times, Tough People and The Taming of a Wild River*. New York: Mikaya Press, 2006.

Weidner Zoehfeld, Kathleen. *Cactus Cafe: A Story of the Sonoran Desert - A Wild Habitats Book*. Norwalk, CT: Soundprints, 1997.

WEBSITES

Arizona Governors' Kids Page

www.azgovernor.gov/AZSpotlight/Kids_Main.asp

Arizona Tourism Guide

www.visitarizona.com

Official Arizona State Website

www.az.gov

ABOUT THE AUTHORS

Kerry Jones Waring is a writer, editor, and communications professional. She lives in Buffalo with her husband and son.

Kathleen Derzipilski is a research editor who specializes in children's nonfiction. She lives in San Diego, California.

Amanda Hudson edits and writes children's books. She lives just outside of New York City, but loves visiting her brother and his wife in Phoenix—especially in March.

Index

Index